MASTERING YOUR MONEY MINDSET:
A GUIDE TO FINANCIAL FREEDOM.

INTRODUCTION:

The secret to reaching financial freedom and leading a prosperous, purposeful life is developing a money mindset. Our views, values, and life experiences have created our complicated and intensely personal connection with money. But a lot of us experience financial stress, debt, and uncertainty, and we often feel powerless over our financial situation.

Why It's Important to Master Your Money Mindset

Living a full life and reaching financial freedom require mastering your money mindset. Understanding your attitudes, convictions, and financial practices will help you:

- Get rid of financial tension and anxiety - Create a good, healthy connection with money - Make wise financial decisions that are consistent with your objectives and values

- Create riches and become financially independent - Lead a prosperous and meaningful life.

CHAPTER 1:

The Study of Money Psychology:

The first step towards mastering your money attitude is realizing the psychological aspects that affect how you relate to money. Numerous elements, such as our upbringing, societal influences, and emotional experiences, influence our views, attitudes, and behaviors about money.

The Influence of Conditioning: Molding Our Attitudes and Actions Regarding Money

We can attribute a great deal of our financial ideas and habits to conditioning. We are socialized from an early age to think and behave a specific way when it comes to money. Our experiences as individuals, as well as our family, society, and media, can all contribute to this conditioning. Realizing the influence of conditioning is crucial to identifying and resisting the limiting thoughts and actions that prevent us from reaching financial independence.

Cultural and Family Conditioning

Our financial attitudes and practices are greatly influenced by our cultural background and family. We pick up financial etiquette by watching and copying our parents, grandparents, and other family members. As an illustration:

Growing up in a home where money is tight might cause us to acquire a scarcity mindset, which is the idea that there is never enough money.
- If we hear the advice to invest and save money all the time, we could start to view money in a riskier way.
- Exposure to debt or excessive spending may cause us to develop similar behaviors.

The cultural norms and beliefs surrounding money that we are exposed to also have an impact.
For example:

While some cultures place more value on spending and having fun, others emphasize saving and being frugal.

- We may be told by artistic beliefs about wealth, success, and status.

Media and Societal Conditioning,

The media and societal influences also shape our fiscal beliefs and actions. We are constantly bombarded with dispatches about plutocrat, wealth, and success. Consider

- announcements promoting luxury goods and services, creating a sense of desire and annuity.
-Social media showcasing others' wealth and material success, fostering comparison and competition.
- News and media outlets immortalizing fear and anxiety around plutocrat and the frugality.

These influences can lead to unrealistic prospects, unhealthy stations, and poor fiscal opinions.

particular gests and Conditioning,

Our particular gests , both positive and negative, also condition our fiscal beliefs and actions. For illustration

- Traumatic gests , similar as fiscal stress or ruin, can lead to fear and avoidance of fiscal opinions.
- felicities or unforeseen wealth can produce a sense of annuity or complacency.

-Successful fiscal opinions or investments can make confidence and encourage threat- taking.

Feting the Power of Conditioning

To master our plutocrat mindset, it's essential to fete and challenge the exertion that shapes our fiscal beliefs and actions. By admitting these influences, we can

- Identify limiting beliefs and replace them with empowering bones
- Develop healthier fiscal habits and actions.
- Make informed, purposeful opinions about plutocrat.
- Break free from conditioning that holds us back from achieving fiscal freedom.

By understanding the power of exertion, we can begin to rewire our smarts and develop a healthier, more empowered relationship with plutocrat.

* **SOCIETAL INFLUENCES** *

Societal influences also play a significant part in shaping our plutocrat mindset. We are constantly bombarded with dispatches that equate wealth with success and happiness. announcements, social media, and the media frequently immortalize the idea that the further plutocrat you have, the better your life will be. This can lead to an unhealthy preoccupation with wealth and material effects.

* Emotional Alarms *

Emotional gests, similar as fiscal stress, debt, or felicities, can also shape our plutocrat mindset. For case, if you've endured fiscal instability in the history, you may have developed a fear of not having enough plutocrat, leading to hoarding or overspending.

* Breaking Free from Limiting Beliefs *

Feting and challenging these limiting beliefs is pivotal to learning your plutocrat mindset. By getting apprehensive of your studies, stations, and actions towards plutocrat, you can be suitable to develop a healthier relationship with plutocrat.

CHAPTER 2

Mindset Shifts- Transforming Your Relationship with plutocrat

learning your plutocrat mindset requires a abecedarian shift in your thinking and beliefs about plutocrat. This chapter will explore the mindset shifts necessary to transfigure your relationship with plutocrat and achieve fiscal freedom.

Mindset Shift 1 From failure to Cornucopia,

The first mindset shift is to move from a failure mindset to an cornucopia mindset. A failure mindset believes that there is noway enough plutocrat, coffers, or openings. In discrepancy, an cornucopia mindset recognizes that there is always enough and that wealth is a mindset, not just a bank account balance.

To borrow an cornucopia mindset

- Practice gratefulness for what you formerly have
- Focus on cornucopia, not warrant
- Embrace the idea that there is always further than enough

Mindset Shift 2 Reframing Negative studies,

The alternate mindset shift is to reframe negative studies and beliefs about plutocrat. Our studies shape our conduct, and negative studies can lead to fiscal struggles. By reframing negative studies, you can

- Challenge limiting beliefs
- Replace negative studies with empowering bones

- Develop a positive mindset

Exemplifications of reframing negative studies

- " I will no way have enough plutocrat" becomes" I've enough plutocrat to meet my requirements, and I am open to new openings."
- " I am not good with plutocrat" becomes" I am able of literacy and managing my finances effectively."

Mindset Shift 3 Embracing a Growth Mindset,

The third mindset shift is to borrow a growth mindset, believing that capacities and intelligence can be developed through hard work, fidelity, and continuity. This mindset is essential for achieving fiscal freedom, as it allows you to

- Embrace challenges and learn from failures
- Develop new chops and knowledge
- Adapt to changing fiscal circumstances

Mindset Shift 4 fastening on Value, Not Just Price,

The fourth mindset shift is to concentrate on value, not just price. This means considering the long- term benefits and value of a purchase, rather than just the original cost.

- Ask yourself" Will this purchase add value to my life?"
- Consider the long- term costs and benefits
- Prioritize investments over charges

Mindset Shift 5 rehearsing tone- Care and tone- Love,

The final mindset shift is to prioritize tone- care and tone- love. When you take care of yourself, you are more equipped to manage your finances and make purposeful opinions about plutocrat.

- Prioritize your physical, emotional, and internal well- being
- Fete your worth and value beyond your fiscal situation
- Embrace tone- compassion and tone- remission

By espousing these mindset shifts, you will be suitable to transfigure your relationship with plutocrat and achieve fiscal freedom. Flash back, learning your plutocrat mindset is a trip, and it's essential to be patient, kind, and compassionate with yourself along the way.

CHAPTER 3

fiscal knowledge- Understanding the Basics:

fiscal knowledge is the foundation of learning your plutocrat mindset. It's essential to understand the basics of particular finance to make informed opinions about your plutocrat. In this chapter, we'll claw into the crucial generalities and principles of fiscal knowledge, furnishing a comprehensive understanding of how to manage your finances effectively.

Key Concept 1 Budgeting,

Budgeting is the process of creating a plan for how you want to allocate your plutocrat towards different charges, savings, and debt prepayment. A budget helps you understand where your plutocrat is going, identify areas for enhancement, and make conscious fiscal opinions.

-, **50/30/20 Rule**, Allocate **50** of your income towards necessary charges(casing, food, serviceability), **30** towards optional spending(entertainment, pursuits), and **20** towards saving and debt prepayment.

-, classify charges, Divide your charges into requirements (casing, food), wants (entertainment, pursuits), and debt prepayment.

-, Prioritize requirements over wants, insure you are meeting your necessary charges before spending on optional particulars.

Key Concept 2 Saving,

Saving is setting aside a portion of your income for short- term and long- term pretensions, extremities, and unanticipated charges. It's essential to prioritize saving to achieve fiscal stability and security.

-, exigency fund, Save three to six months' worth of charges in an fluently accessible savings regard.

-, Short- term pretensions, Allocate plutocrat towards specific pretensions, similar as a holiday
 or down payment on a house.

-, Long- term pretensions, Invest in a withdrawal account or other long- term investment vehicles.

Key Concept 3 Investing,

Investing is growing your wealth by putting your plutocrat into means that induce returns, similar as stocks, bonds, or real estate. Investing can help you achieve long- term fiscal pretensions and make wealth over time.

- , Diversification, Spread your investments across different asset classes to minimize threat.
- , composite interest, utilize the power of time and interest to grow your wealth.
- , Start early, Take advantage of emulsion interest by starting to invest as soon as possible.

Key Concept 4 Debt Management,

Debt operation involves understanding how to adopt plutocrat wisely, manage debt, and produce a plan to come debt-free. It's essential to prioritize debt prepayment to achieve fiscal freedom.

- , Debt snowball, Pay off high- interest debts first, while making minimal payments on other debts.
- , Debt connection, Combine multiple debts into a single loan with a lower interest rate.
- , Credit score, Understand how debt prepayment affects your credit score and long- term fiscal health.

Key Concept 5 Credit,

Credit involves erecting a positive credit history, understanding credit scores, and using credit responsibly. A good credit score can help you qualify for loans and credit cards with favorable interest rates.

- , Credit report, Cover your credit report for crimes and disagreement.

-, Credit score, Aim for a credit score of 700 or advanced.
-, Responsible credit use, Use credit cards wisely and make timely payments.

Key Concept 6 Risk Management,

threat operation involves guarding yourself and your means from unanticipated events, similar as illness, accidents, or natural disasters. It's essential to prioritize threat operation to insure fiscal stability.

-, Insurance, Invest in health, disability, and life insurance to cover yourself and your loved bones
.
-, Emergency fund, Save for unanticipated charges and fiscal shocks.
-, Diversification, Spread your investments across different asset classes to minimize threat.

By understanding these crucial generalities and principles of fiscal knowledge, you will be empowered to make informed opinions about your plutocrat and take control of your fiscal future. Flash back, fiscal knowledge is a lifelong literacy process, and it's essential to stay informed and acclimatize to changing fiscal circumstances.

CHAPTER 4
Investing- Growing Your Wealth

Investing is a pivotal aspect of learning your plutocrat mindset. It's a way to grow your wealth over time, achieve long- term fiscal pretensions, and make a secure fiscal future. In this chapter, we'll claw into the world of investing, exploring the different types of investments, strategies, and stylish practices to help you make informed opinions about your plutocrat.

Type of Investments,

1., Stocks, Also known as equities, stocks represent power in companies, offering implicit for long- term growth.

2., Bonds, Government and commercial bonds offer regular income and fairly lower threat.

3., Real Estate, Investing in property or real estate investment trusts(REITs) can give rental income and long- term appreciation.

4., collective finances, Diversified portfolios of stocks, bonds, or other securities, offering a balanced investment approach.

5., Exchange- Traded finances(ETFs), analogous to collective finances but trade on an exchange like stocks, offering inflexibility.

6., Index finances, Tracking a specific request indicator, similar as the S&P 500, to give broad request exposure.

7., Alternative Investments, Including goods, cryptocurrencies, and barricade finances, for diversification and potentially advanced returns.

Investing Strategies,

1., Diversification, Spread investments across asset classes to minimize threat and maximize returns.

2., Bone- Cost Averaging, Invest a fixed quantum regularly, anyhow of request conditions, to reduce timing pitfalls.

3., Long- term Approach, concentrate on long- term growth, rather than short- term earnings, to ride out request oscillations.

4., Value Investing, Seek unvalued investments with strong fundamentals for implicit long- term growth.

5., Growth Investing, Target investments with high growth eventuality, similar as arising diligence or innovative companies.

Stylish Practices,

1., Set Clear pretensions, Define your investment objects, threat forbearance, and time horizon.
2., Develop a Plan, produce a diversified investment plan, acclimatized to your pretensions and threat profile.
3., Start Early, Take advantage of emulsion interest by starting to invest as soon as possible.
4., Examiner and Acclimate, Regularly review your investments and rebalance your portfolio as demanded.
5., Educate Yourself, Continuously learn about investing and stay informed about request trends and profitable conditions.

Setting Clear pretensions. A pivotal Step in Investing

Setting clear pretensions is a vital step in investing, as it helps you determine the right investment strategy, threat forbearance, and time horizon. Clear pretensions enable you to produce a focused plan, make informed opinions, and measure progress towards achieving your fiscal objects. Let's explore how to set clear pretensions

1., particularity, Define your pretensions precisely, avoiding vague terms like" fiscal security" or" wealth." rather, aim for specific objects, similar as" saving for a down payment on a house" or" erecting a withdrawal fund."

2., Measurability, Quantify your pretensions, making them measurable and trackable. For illustration," saving$ 50,000 for a down payment" or" achieving a 7 periodic return on investment."

3., Achievability, insure your pretensions are realistic and attainable grounded on your fiscal situation, threat forbearance, and time horizon. Avoid setting unachievable pretensions, which can lead to disappointment and frustration.

4., Applicability, Align your pretensions with your values and precedences. Ask yourself," Is this thing important to me?" and" Will achieving this thing truly make a positive impact in my life?"

5., Time- bound, Establish a specific timeframe for achieving your pretensions, whether short- term(lower than 3 times), medium- term(3- 7 times), or long- term(further than 7 times). This helps produce a sense of urgency and focus.

Examples of clear goals:

Exemplifications of clear pretensions

-" I want to save $20,000 for a marriage within the next 2 years, with a yearly investment of $800."
-" I aim to make a withdrawal fund of $500,000 in the coming 20 years, contributing $500 yearly."
-" I want to increase my net worth by 20% within the coming 5 years, through a combination of investments and debt reduction."

By setting clear pretensions, you will produce a roadmap for your investing trip, guiding your opinions and helping you stay focused on what matters most – achieving your fiscal bournes.

CHAPTER 5

Practical Tips and Tools- Actionable Tips and coffers for perfecting Financial Habits.

learning your plutocrat mindset requires practical tools and strategies to ameliorate fiscal habits, track charges, and manage plutocrat effectively. In this chapter, we'll give practicable tips and coffers to help you achieve fiscal success.

Practicable Tips:

1. **Track Charges Recording;** every sale, no matter how small, it's pivotal to understanding spending habits and relating

areas for enhancement. Use a tablet, spreadsheet, or app like Mint or Personal Capital to log charges. classify charges into requirements(casing, food, serviceability) and wants(entertainment, pursuits) to prioritize spending.

2. produce a Budget, Set fiscal pretensions and allocate income consequently; prioritizing requirements over wants. Consider the50/30/20 rule 50 for musts, 30 for optional spending, and 20 for saving and debt prepayment. Acclimate the proportions grounded on individual circumstances.

3. Automate Savings Set up automatic transfers to savings and investment accounts. Take advantage of employer- matched withdrawal accounts like 401(k) or IRA. Use apps like Digit or Acorns to automatically save small quantities.

4. Pay Off High- Interest Debt Focus on barring high- interest debt, similar as credit card balances. Consider debt connection, balance transfer, or snowball styles. Negotiate with creditors for lower interest rates or payment plans.

5. make an Emergency Fund Save 3- 6 months' worth of charges for unanticipated events like auto repairs or medical bills. Use a separate savings regard or a high- yield savings app like Marcus or Discover.

6. Monitor Credit Reports Regularly review credit reports to descry crimes and fraud. Request free reports from(link unapproachable) and disagreement any inaccuracies.

7. Avoid Lifestyle Creep Avoid adding spending as income rises, rather directing redundant finances towards savings and investments.

8. Take Advantage of Tax- Advantaged Accounts use duty-remitted accounts like 401(k), IRA, or Roth IRA for withdrawal savings, and duty-free accounts like HSA or 529 plans for specific charges.

9. Invest Wisely Consider low- cost indicator finances or ETFs, and diversify your portfolio to minimize threat. Use robo- counsels like Betterment or Wealthfront for automated investment operation.

10. Educate Yourself Continuously learn about particular finance, investing, and plutocrat operation to make informed opinions. Follow fiscal experts, bloggers, and podcasters for guidance and alleviation.

fiscal Apps and Software:

1. Mint Personal finance app shadowing charges, creating budgets, and setting fiscal pretensions.

2. Personal Capital Financial operation tool shadowing income, charges, and investments.

3. YNAB(You Need a Budget) Budgeting app helping druggies manage finances and achieve fiscal pretensions.

4. Credit Karma: Free credit monitoring and reporting service.

5. Quicken Personal finance software shadowing charges, creating budgets, and managing investments.

6. Turbo Tax medication software helping druggies optimize duty returns.

7. Digit Savings app automatically transferring small quantities from checking to savings.

8. make use of Investment app rounding up purchases and investing spare change.

9. store Investment app allowing druggies to invest small quantities in ETFs.

10. Clarity Money Financial operation app shadowing charges, income, and investments.

Other Tools and coffers

1. Spreadsheets Microsoft Excel or Google wastes for budgeting and expenditure shadowing.

2. Piggy Banks Physical or digital holders for saving coins and bills.

3. Cash Envelopes Divide charges into orders, using cash for optional spending.

4. Financial counsels Professional guidance for investment and fiscal planning.

5. Online Forums Communities participating knowledge and gests, similar as Reddit's r/ personalfinance.

6. Books and Podcasts Educational coffers like" The Total plutocrat Makeover" and" The Dave Ramsey Show".

7. Budgeting Workbooks Printable or digital workbooks guiding druggies through budgeting and expenditure shadowing.

8. Financial Planners Professionals creating individualized fiscal plans and investment strategies.

9. Automated Savings Tools Apps like Qapital or Savings Spree helping druggies save plutocrat automatically.

10. Financial Education Courses Online courses tutoring particular finance, investing, and plutocrat operation.

By enforcing these practical tips and exercising the colorful tools and coffers available, you will be well on your way to perfecting fiscal habits, shadowing charges, and managing plutocrat more effectively. Flash back, learning your plutocrat mindset is a nonstop process, and staying informed and visionary is crucial to achieving long- term fiscal success.

CHAPTER 6

Threat operation- guarding Your Wealth and Well- being:

threat operation is an essential aspect of learning your plutocrat mindset, as it helps you prepare for and alleviate implicit fiscal pitfalls. In this chapter, we'll explore the colorful types of fiscal pitfalls, strategies for managing threat, and stylish practices for guarding your wealth and well- being.

Types of Financial pitfalls

1. * request threat * The threat of investments declining in value due to request oscillations.
2. * Credit threat * The threat of lenders defaulting on loans or debt scores.
3. * Liquidity threat * The threat of not being suitable to pierce cash or liquidate means snappily enough.
4. * Affectation threat * The threat of affectation eroding the purchasing power of your plutocrat.
5. * Interest Rate threat * The threat of changes in interest rates affecting your investments or debt.
6. * Currency threat * The threat of oscillations in currency values affecting transnational investments.
7. * functional threat * The threat of fraud, cyber attacks, or other functional failures.

Strategies For Managing Threat

1. * Diversification * Spreading investments across asset classes to reduce exposure to any one threat.
2. * Asset Allocation * Allocating means grounded on threat forbearance, pretensions, and time horizon.
3. * Hedging * Using derivations or other instruments to alleviate specific pitfalls.
4. * Insurance * Transferring threat to insurance companies to cover against unanticipated events.
5. * Regular Portfolio Rebalancing * Periodically reviewing and conforming investments to maintain an optimal threat profile.

Stylish Practices for Risk Management

1. * Develop a Risk Management Plan * Identify implicit pitfalls and produce a plan to alleviate them.
2. * Examine and Review * Regularly review your investments and threat exposure.
3. * Diversify and Hedge * Use diversification and hedging strategies to reduce threat.
4. * ensure and cover * Use insurance and other protection mechanisms to transfer threat.
5. * Educate Yourself * Continuously learn about threat operation and stay informed about request conditions.

Fresh Tips:

1. * Assess Your threat Forbearance * Understand your comfort position with threat and acclimate your strategy consequently.
2. * Use threat operation Tools * use tools like stop- loss orders and options to manage threat.
3. * Diversify Across Asset Classes * Spread investments across stocks, bonds, real estate, and other asset classes.
4. * Consider Alternative Investments * Explore indispensable investments like private equity or barricade finances to diversify your portfolio.
5. * Seek Professional Advice * Consult with a fiscal counsel or threat operation expert to get substantiated guidance.

By understanding and managing fiscal pitfalls, you can cover your wealth and well- being, and achieve long- term fiscal success. Flash back, risk operation is an ongoing process that requires regular monitoring and adaptations to insure optimal results.

CHAPTER 7

Case Studies and Success Stories Real- Life exemplifications of learning Your plutocrat Mindset:

In this chapter, we'll claw into real- life exemplifications and success stories of individualities who have applied the principles outlined in this ebook. These case studies will give alleviation and provocation for compendiums to apply the principles in their own lives, demonstrating the transformative power of learning your plutocrat mindset.

Case Study 1: Sarah's Journey to Financial Freedom

Sarah, a 35 years old marketing professional, was floundering to make ends meet. Despite her decent income, she set up herself drowning in debt and living stipend to stipend. After discovering the principles outlined in this ebook, Sarah committed to transubstantiating her fiscal life. She started by creating a budget, prioritizing her spending, and investing in a diversified portfolio. Within a time, Sarah paid off her debt, erected an exigency fund, and began saving for her long- term pretensions. years later, Sarah is debt-free, financially independent, and living a life true to her values.

Case Study 2 Alex's Path to Wealth Creation

Alex, a 28 years old entrepreneur, had always pictured of erecting wealth. After applying the principles outlined in this ebook, Alex started investing in real estate, tip- paying stocks, and a small business. Through disciplined savings, smart investing, and duty optimization, Alex erected a substantial net worth. Years later, Alex is a successful business proprietor, investor, and philanthropist, living a life of purpose and fiscal freedom.

Case Study 3 Rachel's Transformation from Financial Stress to Serenity

Rachel, a 40- years old single mama, was overwhelmed by fiscal stress. Despite her stylish sweats, she plodded to make ends meet and give for her family. After discovering the principles outlined in this ebook, Rachel began to transfigure her fiscal life. She created a budget, prioritized her spending, and invested in a diversified portfolio. Within two times, Rachel paid off her debt, erected an exigency fund, and started saving for her children's education. Years later, Rachel is financially secure, stress-free, and living a life filled with purpose and joy.

Success Story 1: From ruin to Financial Freedom

John, a 50- year-old businessman, filed for ruin after a series of unfortunate events. Devastated and feeling defeated, John accepted he would noway recover. still, after applying the principles outlined in this ebook, John started rebuilding his fiscal life. He created a budget, invested in a diversified portfolio, and concentrated on erecting multiple income aqueducts. Within five years, John paid off his debt, erected a substantial net worth, and achieved fiscal freedom. John is a successful entrepreneur, investor, and philanthropist, living a life of purpose and fiscal serenity.

Success Story 2: A youthful Couple's Journey to Early Retirement

Emily and Mike, both 32, were determined to retire beforehand and live a life of fiscal freedom. After applying the principles outlined in this ebook, they started investing in a diversified portfolio, maximizing their duty- advantaged accounts, and erecting multiple income aqueducts. Within 10 years, Emily and Mike achieved fiscal independence, retiring from their commercial jobs to pursue their heartstrings. moment, they travel the world, levy, and live a life of purpose and fiscal freedom.

These case studies and success stories demonstrate the transformative power of learning your plutocrat mindset. By applying the principles outlined in this ebook, individualities can overcome fiscal struggles, make wealth, and achieve a life of purpose and fiscal freedom. Flash back, learning your plutocrat mindset is a trip, and every small step counts. Take alleviation from these stories and start your own trip moment!

CHAPTER 8

Nonstop literacy- Empowering Yourself for Long- Term Financial Success

This e-book has handed a solid foundation for understanding the principles of fiscal freedom, but the trip does not end then. nonstop literacy is essential to achieving long- term fiscal success, and this chapter will encourage and empower you to continue your fiscal education beyond this ebook.

Stimulant to Continue Financial Education

learning your plutocrat mindset is a lifelong process. The fiscal geography is constantly evolving, and new strategies and ways crop every time. To stay ahead of the game, it's pivotal to commit to nonstop literacy. By doing so, you'll

- Stay informed about request trends and profitable changes
- upgrade your fiscal chops and knowledge
- Adapt to new challenges and openings
- Achieve long- term fiscal freedom and peace of mind.

Recommended Readings

1. "The Total Money Makeover" by Dave Ramsey
2. "Your Money or Your Life" by Vicki Robin and Joe Dominguez
3. "The Simple Path to Wealth" by JL Collins
4. "The Intelligent Investor" by Benjamin Graham
5. "The Little Book of Common Sense Investing" by John C. Bogle

These books offer valuable insights, practical advice, and inspiring stories to help you deepen your understanding of personal finance and investing.

Online Courses

1. Coursera - "Personal Finance" by University of Michigan
2. Udemy - "Mastering Personal Finance"
3. edX - "Finance for Non-Financial Professionals"
4. LinkedIn Learning (formerly Lynda.com) - "Personal Finance Fundamentals"
5. The Financial Diet - "Financial Freedom Course"

These online courses provide structured learning experiences, interactive exercises, and expert instruction to enhance your financial knowledge and skills.

Networking Opportunities

1. Attend financial conferences and seminars
2. Join online forums and communities (e.g., Reddit's r/personalfinance)
3. Connect with financial professionals and mentors
4. Participate in local investment clubs or study groups
5. Follow financial experts and bloggers on social media

Networking with like-minded individuals and financial experts will help you stay motivated, learn from others' experiences, and gain access to valuable resources and insights.

In Conclusion,
Mastering your money mindset is a continuous journey, and this ebook has provided a solid foundation for your financial education. Remember, the key to long-term financial success lies in ongoing learning, self-improvement, and adaptation. Embrace the mindset of continuous learning, and you'll be empowered to achieve financial freedom and peace of mind. Keep learning, growing, and thriving on your financial journey!

CONCLUSION -

Mastering Your Money Mindset: A Journey to Financial Freedom

Congratulations on completing "Mastering Your Money Mindset: A Guide to Financial Freedom"! This ebook has provided a comprehensive roadmap to help you transform your financial life and achieve lasting prosperity. As we conclude this journey together, let's recap the key takeaways and reflect on the significance of mastering your money mindset.

KEY TAKEAWAYS:

1. Understanding your money mindset and its impact on financial decisions
2. Setting clear financial goals and creating a personalized plan
3. Managing debt, building credit, and optimizing financial tools
4. Investing wisely, diversifying, and harnessing compound interest
5. Cultivating a long-term perspective, discipline, and patience
6. Embracing continuous learning and self-improvement

These principles and strategies form the foundation of a healthy financial mindset, empowering you to make informed decisions, overcome obstacles, and achieve your goals.

Final Thoughts:

Mastering your money mindset is a journey, not a destination. It requires commitment, resilience, and a willingness to learn and adapt. By applying the principles outlined in this ebook, you'll be better equipped to navigate the complexities of personal finance, make informed decisions, and achieve lasting financial freedom.

Remember, financial freedom is a state of mind, not just a financial status. It's the ability to live life on your own terms, pursue your passions, and make a meaningful impact. By mastering your money mindset, you'll unlock the doors to a brighter financial future, filled with purpose, joy, and peace of mind.

ENCOURAGEMENT:

As you embark on this journey, remember that you're not alone. Millions of people have achieved financial freedom, and you can too. Stay committed, stay disciplined, and stay patient. Celebrate your small wins, learn from your setbacks, and keep moving forward.

Embrace the power of continuous learning, and stay curious about personal finance and investing. Surround yourself with like-minded individuals, seek guidance from financial experts, and stay informed about market trends and economic changes.

Most importantly, believe in yourself and your ability to master your money mindset. You possess the strength, resilience, and determination to achieve greatness. Go forth, conquer your financial challenges, and unlock the doors to a life of financial freedom and prosperity!

"FAREWELL, AND HAPPY JOURNEYING"